We Are the
Young Magicians

Barnard New Women Poets Series

Edited by Christopher Baswell
and Celeste Schenck

We Are the
Young Magicians

RUTH FORMAN

With an Introduction by

Cherríe Moraga

Beacon Press

Boston

Beacon Press
25 Beacon Street
Boston, Massachusetts 02108-2892

Beacon Press books
are published under the auspices of
the Unitarian Universalist Association of Congregations.

99 98 97 96   8 7 6 5 4 3

The Barnard New Women Poets Series
is supported in part by funds
given in memory of Barbara and Marilyn Meyers.

Text design by Diane Bigda

Library of Congress Cataloging-in-Publication Data

Forman, Ruth.
    We are the young magicians / Ruth Forman; with an
introduction by Cherríe Moraga.
        p.   cm.—(Barnard new women poets series)
    ISBN 0-8070-6820-9.—ISBN 0-8070-6821-7 (pbk.)
    1. Afro-Americans—Poetry.   I. Title.   II. Series.
PS3556.07334W4   1993
811'.54—dc20
                                                    92-37807
                                                        CIP

*For Herbie
and all those who've made
this book possible*

Contents

We Are the Young Magicians

Acknowledgments

Grateful acknowledgment is made to the editors of the journals in which these poems first appeared:

"Young Cornrows Callin out the Moon":
Afrikan Student Literary Magazine 2, bk. 2 (Spring 1991)
In the Company of Poets Magazine (April/May 1992)

"Poetry Should Ride the Bus":
Poetry for the People What Now? (Fall 1991)
In the Company of Poets Magazine (April/May 1992)

"What Will It Take?":
Smell This 2, no. 2 (Spring 1991)

"For Your Information," "3:59," "Top Gun," "I Did Not Pee My Pants Somebody Else Did":
Poetry for the People in a Time of War (Spring 1991)

"Labels for 99Cent":
Afrikan Student Literary Magazine 2, bk. 1 (Fall 1990)

"In a Darkroom":
Afrikan Student Literary Magazine 1, bk. 2 (Spring 1990)

"I Will Speak Genius to Myself":
Afrikan Student Literary Magazine 1, bk. 1 (Fall 1989)
Smell This 1, no. 1 (Spring 1990)

"The Call":
Smell This 1, no. 1 (Spring 1990)

"A Split Tree Still Grows":
In the Company of Poets Magazine (April/May 1992)

"Up Sister":
Smell This 1, no. 1 (Spring 1990)
Afrikan Student Literary Magazine 1, bk. 1 (Fall 1989)

Introduction

Cherríe Moraga

"*To be young, gifted and Black,*" in the words of Lorraine Hansberry, this is Ruth Forman, twenty-four years old and "slammin." Her poems speak truth, a truth that seldom appears on the pages of "literary" publications, and yet emerges from one of the finest literary traditions this country has known. In these pages, you will find the sensuality of an Alice Walker, the revolutionary fervor of a June Jordan, the mule-stubbornness of a Zora Neale Hurston. How blessed Ruth Forman is to claim these women as legacy. In their name she writes knowing, like they, that she was not meant to write; and therefore, she writes for all those censored and forgotten . . . and she defines the terms.

> this poem slammin this poem black
> n nobody tell me nothin cuz i said it
> this poem be us n
> this poem be poetry

Ruth Forman is an original voice, a thoroughly twenty-first-century poet who anticipates a world transformed by the "genius" of her generation. "This poem be us." Ruth Forman's vision is unabashedly collective. Her poems bear witness to the new woman writer, the "young magician" who "spin[s] unalone" in the creation of a "new silk"—the Black and beautifully female fabric of a life.

To Ruth Forman, poetry is the "black magic," inherited from childhood "brownstone steps" on "South Philly summer" evenings. It is "Oz" found in the cracks of sidewalks. It is, as Audre Lorde says, "not a luxury." Poetry is critical to the good sense and health of a people. It is substance. It "should ride the bus / in a fat woman's Safeway bag / between the greens n chicken wings / to be served with Tuesday's dinner." It is ordinary, as ordinary as "drop[ping] by a sweet potato pie, ask[ing] about the grandchildren / n sit[ting] through a whole photo album / on a orange

plastic-covered La-Z-Boy with no place to go." And finally, "poetry
should . . . not be so educated that it don't stop in / every now n
then to sit on the porch / and talk about the comins and goins of
the world."

Ruth Forman's poetry is a poetry of necessity. She writes with
an informed urgency against censors (both real and imagined), al-
ways lurking, always waiting to subvert the sistapoet's purpose. If
you lose your pen, "it is not your pen you are looking for / it is
your tongue." She urges us to write, write with "the blood of your
finger" if you must, but write. *It is that necessary.*

> poetry is always for the people
> and it is always a time of war

The backdrop to *We Are the Young Magicians* is a war whose
perpetrators project a kaleidoscope of contradictory images:
fatigue-wearing "thank you maam" soldierboys returning from the
Persian Gulf colliding with fatigue-wearing "oozie-lookin brothas"
catcalling to the "honeys" at a streetlight. Of the Gulf War, Ruth
Forman protests, "well i did not pee my pants / somebody else
did / n i don't know who n they put it in my bedroom." She's no-
body's fool. She will not be complicitous in a war she did not cre-
ate—in or out of the bedroom. That same Black womanish wisdom
draws a lucid connection between the male seduction in the sim-
ple gesture of lighting a woman's cigarette and the military /
media seduction of burning up oil fields in the Gulf. "Lies come on
matches," she warns. The match cover with its "instant credit"
number on the back becomes conspiracy, makes us all unwitting
accomplices to the crime of a consumerist society that sells vio-
lence like cigarettes.

> n all the time i'm thinkin of the videos
> . . . .
> cuz it's kinda in style for lil honeys
> to be all over somebody big who look like
> somethin white people call the police on
> cuz they jus look wrong /

n honeys be all over them in like twos n threes
sometimes / in the videos / i know you seen them /
....
n they seen on tv that it's kinda in style to hop on over
to somethin that will fuck you up in a minute /
n they didn't really know it would be like that /
tryin to find a way out from where they're at /
n somebody drive by offerin all this kinda shit /
n they think it's kinda cool cuz you know /
on tv it's kinda cool to be a soldier / kinda in style /
n the big dealers just sittin up there /
thinkin you be their lil honey
or somethin / n i wonder why
they think i be down for somethin like that / why
we be down for somethin like that

The lies engineered by mainstream media are contrasted with the brutal reality of the videotaped Rodney King beating; but here, Black America and all of America, including a twelve-person jury, are told "what they seen is not what they seen." And SistaRuth's pen grows in its revolutionary promise: "you are the blood we need / . . . the cross burns my front yard n smoke over the roof chants your name." We know now that this young poet magician will become a soldier of a very different breed. This war leaves no time for natural birthings. "In a womb of razor black glass/O Truth sings without mercy without and within / you cannot resist any longer." And the revolutionary is born "cesarean section," cut out to join her Black army, to fight this war of greed and deception.

Oh and is Ruth Forman's poetry ever Black! A black that "don blanket" her from seeing what she must as the poet visionary magician. A black that is by its essence a call for justice. "Blackisblackisblackisblack. / Pitch black." And steeped in the essence of that uncompromising identity, she refuses any rigid fundamentalism. When a brother artist tries to convince her that all white men are devils, she responds:

The balance of this earth
is not dependent upon the absence of devils

it is dependent upon the presence of angels and
spirit, not color, determines.

There is no naiveté in this work. She knows the enemy's name; all
that would call her ugly or unintelligent. Ruth Forman is fully con-
scious of her place amongst a new breed of writer / revolutionary.
These "young, gifted and Black" artists and thinkers are the survi-
vors of an education bent on securing their silence, their acquies-
cence, their inferiority complexes, and ultimately their suicides.
She calls herself "genius" in the name of all her sisters and broth-
ers.

> . . . I know that my face is authentic
> my mind is authentic
> my words are authentic
> so I will speak genius to myself.

She is the "cigarette burn" in the face of academia. Its unyielding
scar.

In spite of her education, Ruth Forman's poetic and political
world allows no room for elitism. She understands that the differ-
ence between the sister that's made it and she who hasn't is just a
car. There is no fake sense of family in these pages. They are
stained with blood ties formed by a history of slavery and a living
racial memory, forging a sister / brotherhood of mahogany, pecan,
oak, ebony with "roots / held tight to [the] soul / nothing could
shake them." The splittings of racism can never wholly eradicate
this collective consciousness, the roots of African American sur-
vival.

> Look at me
> I am we
> we are old
> we are the beginning of life
> we survive the seasons
> we are the new buds upon the highest branches

The greatest passion of Ruth Forman's voice emerges in her
love of Black womanhood. Here the sensuality of her childhood

memories of "crush blueberries / . . . the lil ones / redblue firm and sweet sweet" take shape in the full bodies of her magician sisters "lookin so good / cockroaches ask you to step on em / sos they can see heaven / befo / and after they die . . ." In the poem, "Momma" we learn that the poet's celebration of Black female sensuality was initiated by her mother's presence. "You taste like thick cream and almonds in your prayers / for God to watch over your children."

The "young magicians" of Ruth Forman's collection are *blues women,* decidedly unromantic, with "low make sense kinda voice[s]" that "sound sooo sexy." The poet knows she's got one, too. She looks to no man for salvation, but to the sister and the poem which is the "hand [that] reaches in that darkness / and pulls you up by the waist / even when you don't want to go / cuz it has faith in you." The young magicians are women of color sisters / poets / warriors / writers who have learned to transform the "grey concrete" of urban despair to "yellow brick roads" of imagination, opportunity, and future.

At its heart, *We Are the Young Magicians* speaks to a complete ethical transformation of society, where what is considered worthless by some, like pennies discarded on the sidewalk, "dark n ol n ugly," are licked by the acid of Black female tongues and "glow back out sunset color." *We'll be holding the cards,* Ruth Forman warns. These young magicians will change the name and shape of the worthy.

As you open this book, open your nostrils. The poet invites, "smell / in the darkness / our power."

October 1992
San Francisco

We Spin Unalone

Young Cornrows
Callin Out the Moon

we don have no backyard
frontyard neither
we got black magic n brownstone steps
when the sun go down

we don have no backyard
no sof grass rainbow kites mushrooms butterflies
we got South Philly summer
when the sun go down

cool after lemonade n black eye peas
full after ham hocks n hot pepper greens
corn bread coolin on the stove
n more to watch than tv

we got double dutch n freeze tag n kickball
so many place to hide n seek n
look who here Punchinella Punchinella
look who here Punchinella inna zoo

we got the ice cream man

we got the corner store
red cream pop
red nails Rick James the Bump the Rock
n we know all the cheers

we got pretty lips
we got callous feet healthy thighs n ashy knees
we got fiiine brothas we r fiiine sistas
n
we got attitude

we hold mamma knees when she snap the naps out
we got gramma tell her not to pull so hard
we got sooo cleeen cornrows when she finish
n corn bread cool on the stove

So you know
we don really want no backyard
frontyard neither
cuz we got to call out the moon
wit black magic n brownstone steps

Waitin on Summer

Daddy
is hot butter corn bread in the winter
n a big size 44 belt
chasin me round the kitchen table

Daddy
is thunder with the brothers
light rain with the sisters
n lightning with me n Richie
if we dance on the living room floor

Daddy
is smooth blue sky
in his Sedan de Ville
on Sunday afternoon

Daddy
is hot butter corn bread in the winter
pork n beans n boiled hot dogs
but when the thermometer hit 75
n it's time to barbecue
n times is good
n me n Richie don't run in the house

Daddy
is cool cool lemonade
with the peel
jus floatin on top

On Ma Way

Um finna go find me Oz
the crack in the sidewalk say
come on this way
you a pretty lil girl
you got rubber on yr sneakers so go head n jump
but watch out for the dandelion by yr right foot

Um six n um smart
enough to understan dandelions
she look so nice in my braid
she say she nobody weed

We gonna follow the sun
she gonna take us to Oz
she kiss the sidewalk n dandelion n me
we feel so good we get glowin
we feel so nice we start jumpin

We three n on our way
to i don know where we goin
but this here is ma yellow brick road
n there might be no Oz
but ma feet still be jumpin

I Remember Four

Herbie, Johanna, Richie, Ruthie
four was a good number
tumbling smiles on the living room rug
One tug on your red plaid shirt
Give me a ride Herbie!
and I was seven feet tall

Four
or is it three plus one in memory
but one in memory can be so strong
I remember four
and try to forget September
you sitting on a park bench
.38 on tangent temple
one tug on the trigger
Give me a ride Lord

Four
or is it three plus one in memory
but one in memory can be so strong
you who made me smile
seven feet high on your shoulders
just holding your big rough hand

Aienka with the Colors

she
crush blueberries
not fat n mushy in the grocery store
but the lil ones
redblue firm n sweet sweet
she
the blood seeping from an ashy knee
pulled from the concrete
Kool-Aid cherry mixed with grape
n strawberry rocket pop wrapped in dusk
right before the streetlight turn on
red wine at candlelight which she never had but wish on
once in a while when her heart get thirsty
blackberry lipstick she like to wear
when Mamma not lookin
on her way down the step past the trees
whistlin at her back
after catchin her sweat
Aienka with the colors somewhere between sunset and
    dusk
n night jus comin on

A Dragonfly's Wing

Momma the strawberries are gone too quickly
n with them the steps n paint peeling
we used to sit n watch the termites
with ice cream at our chin

Momma what color was the jump rope
n what did we sing in the kitchen
the fireflies crawl out of the jars again
n I cannot find the top

Momma you do not touch my head anymore
the pick is in the bathroom drawer
afros are out of style
I do not have a camera to hold you n me n the strawberries
my eyes are not used to summertime without you

Poetry Should Ride the Bus

poetry should hopscotch in a polka dot dress
wheel cartwheels
n hold your hand
when you walk past the yellow crackhouse

poetry should wear bright red lipstick
n practice kisses in the mirror
for all the fine young men with fades
shootin craps around the corner

poetry should dress in fine plum linen suits
n not be so educated that it don't stop in
every now n then to sit on the porch
and talk about the comins and goins of the world

poetry should ride the bus
in a fat woman's Safeway bag
between the greens n chicken wings
to be served with Tuesday's dinner

poetry should drop by a sweet potato pie
ask about the grandchildren
n sit through a whole photo album
on a orange plastic covered La-Z-Boy with no place to go

poetry should sing red revolution love songs
that massage your scalp
and bring hope to your blood
when you think you're too old to fight

yeah
poetry should whisper electric blue magic
all the years of your life
never forgettin to look you in the soul
every once in a while
n smile

If You Lose Your Pen

and all you find is a broken pencil on the floor
and the pencil has no sharpener
and the sharpener is in the store
and your pocket has no money

and if you look again
and all you find is a black Bic
and the Bic you need is green

and if it appears beneath the mattress of your couch
but the couch is dirty and you suddenly want to clean
beneath the pillows
but you have no vacuum and the vacuum is in the store
and your pocket has no money

it is not your pen you are looking for

it is your tongue and those who speak with it
your grandmothers and doves and ebony spiders
hovering the corners of your throat

it is your tongue
and if you cannot find your tongue
do not go looking for the cat
you know you will not find her
she is in the neighbor's kitchen eating Friskies
she is in the neighbor's yard making love

if you cannot find your tongue do not look for it
for you are so busy looking it cannot find you
the doves are getting dizzy and your grandmothers annoyed
be still and let them find you
they will come when they are ready

and when they are
it will not matter if your pockets are empty
if you write with a green Bic or a black Bic
or the blood of your finger
you will write
you will write

This Poem

for Lisa

gonna be so slammin
dogs start barkin at nobody passin by
n everybody on Wall Street stop what they doin n say
damn
this poem gonna be so bad
lil girls don want no candy
lil boys hush n mamma don't get a headache
this poem gonna be so bad
daddy get home from work early
jus to dance wit mamma before dinner

this poem be barbecue hot hot hot n red cream soda
this poem be old jeans n new underwear
this poem be Cadillacs n ruby lips n goin out
this poem be curly curly hair
this poem be cowrie shells n kinte
this poem be Haitian dance n sage burnin
black black thick thick sweet sweet
n orange purple sunset when the car break down

this poem ride AC Transit
n this poem say a prayer for women n wheelchairs
alone at night
n this poem know you gave your lover alla you
n the thief won't give you back no pieces
but this poem say
girl your river's everflowin everlastin
so keep on steppin strong sister
this poem say God don love the repo man
n night sticks n broken ribs n bullet holes
in the left shoulder of a strong strong back

this poem be me talkin bout this poem be me talkin bout
your dog barkin
this poem be me talkin bout your lover laughin
talkin bout you talkin bout you in this poem
be you laughin you black you thick
you sweet sweet honey on my pancakes in the mornin
sunrise in your fingers singing
what this poem gonna be
n i don care if i sound like um stuck in the sixties
this poem slammin this poem black
n nobody tell me nothin cuz i said it
this poem be us n
this poem be poetry

We Spin Unalone

If this don't flow cool
maybe i am not the river
if it don't call moons
maybe i am not the dance
if it don't spin gold
maybe i am not the griot

but who will rise the dragons

i am jus a chile coming woman soon
i need to love my breasts
low crying chestnuts
i need to love my hair
forest blooming thick
i need to let go babies
hid beneath my tongue

maybe you are the one
with a moon glowing in yr throat

maybe you are not the one
to sing me to the perfect places

but i need canon i need chorus
i need solos hot n roasted
in the palm of our mouth
n dragons woke from hallways

if you are not the one
who will rise the dragons

I call baby wings from yr throat
to crawl from onyx eggs beneath yr tongue n fly

n if they fly
n if you find yr voice new silk
spiral hair n chestnuts loved n shy moons dancing
it's cuz we spin unalone
at the rate of the earth's rotation
n our own laws of gravity

Cesarean Section

For Your Information

poetry is always for the people
and it is always a time of war

I Did Not Pee My Pants
Somebody Else Did

when you were 9
did you break your neighbor's window
did you pee your pants n hide them behind the bed
tell a lie when your mommy found them
say they were not yours

well the shame is not the same
though maybe somebody would want me to think it is
wrong i don't agree
with this war
well somebody's putting something over on me

those welcome home commercials
smile nightly between sitcoms
Delta lets the soldiers fly home for about a dollar
n that baseball manager says
"welcome home
we r real proud of you
you can have my front row seat anytime"
if i don't say
"welcome home i'm proud of you boys"
i'm not supportive
well i am
i jus never wanted them to go in the first place
n all i can think is
how can they get a front row seat
if they don't have his number
or address

the shame is not the same
though maybe somebody would want me to think it is
well i did not pee my pants
somebody else did
n i don't know who n they put it in my bedroom

3:59

n the black don blanket
the street light through the crack in the curtain
n the black don blanket
the drip drip in the bathtub
n the black don blanket
them numbers 3:59 on my clock radio

i see commercials for Sleep-eze n Unisom
run more n more
tween nightly war updates on channel 7
n i could sure use some a them lil white pills
but i don really got the money

i stare down the radio
n guess what second 3:59 gonna flip to 4:00
my pillow get more flat n greasy
my head turn lef n right
the street light force its way
through the crack in the curtain
i wonder why i can't sleep

well maybe um the night watchguard
n somebody forget to tell me
cuz they too busy watchin
Nintendo wars on channel 4
n exclusive coverage at 6 n 11
updates every half hour
run more n more
tween them white commercials
of lil fake peace pills

i don have none on my night stand n
the black don blanket my anger

cuz my pajamas twist my legs n i can't move again
deep breath
don bring my soul to sleep
don bring my eyes to close
peace don come tonight

channel 5 smiles tempt me
take them lil white pills
suffocate ya mind
valium ya conscious

but i won have none on my night stand
somethin tells me
my sleep ain comin for a reason
somethin tells me
um a night watchguard

cuz if everybody sleep
who be the one to call out in the black for justice?

Lucky Strikes

My matches offer me instant credit
         major bank cards
         signature loans
for two dollars a minute
on the 24-hr cash line
"close cover before striking"

who really believe
they can get out of debt
by calling a number on five-cent matches

we burn each other tryin to get over
n people in so much trouble
they about to call
this number
knowin it's not gonna do them any great favors
but so hopeless that they do it anyway
tryin to make money
from some matches
they get at the liquor store

what's goin on
who is at the end of the number
and who lets them do this anyway
i will tell my daughter
"Baby, don't smoke" cuz
lies come with cigarettes
         smiles
         and a lighter
lies come with matches
         burning oil fields
         and American clean-up teams

Bush knows the rules
"close cover before striking"
so no one will see the truth
just like he bargained away American hostages
so Reagan could win his election

lies come on matches
they do
I see them in my hand every day
lies come with fires
and sometimes people light them on purpose
sometimes people light the match with a smile
sometimes not
but they burn you on purpose
they burn you for sex
they burn you for money
they burn you for insurance
they burn you for oil
and then say you did it
i don't know
i didn't see them smile
but I saw the black smoke on tv

I'm not gonna let
my daughter play with matches
and I'm not gonna let
my daughter smoke
because
contrary to popular belief
American strikes ain't lucky

White Flower Day
or
Macy's from the Top Down

Floral prints in this year
bloom on baby doll dresses
dance cotton
in this year of death

Escalate down
to where summer on racks
outshines scenes of grey smoke
clinging to the back of our heads

Escalate down
to the cologne counter
we spray Estee Lauder White Linen on our necks
to cover up the smell of flesh
and
at the cosmetic counter
rub pale summer frosts for our lips
on the back of our hands
we are so tired of the color red

so tired from fluorescent
commission smiles
video fashion
we leave with full shiny handled bags
and wonder
how we charged so much
and still don't feel
pretty

In the Corner on the Floor

i can't understand
why should i want to be here
and where should i be
and am i supposed to be upset anymore
if there is still a war going on
and is there
and why am i still afraid

next is the fact that i don't understand
what's going on
and i'm trying to understand so hard you know
trying to understand
what happens when the war is over
and is it over
and why is my brother not home yet

next is the fact that i was late to my apartment today
cuz i wasn't sure if here is where i wanted to be
but there was no place else to go
so i locked the door behind me

next is the fact that i'm trying to watch CNN
but i jus get more confused
and i don't know what's going on
i don't know how should i feel
i don't know where should i be
so i sit myself in the corner on the floor
and i rock myself back and forth
and think what a sorry excuse i am

Top Gun

arrive in San Francisco
after six-hour flight
brush-cut fresh
from basic training
he
reach
for his duffel bag

a woman his mother age
sit two seats to my left
she
peach lipstick strawberry blonde bun
look up n say
"You boys are doing a wonderful job"

he
flash down a thank you maam smile n look at
me
to second the motion
that i too am proud of such a white boy

but
i find no words to say
n embarrass by my silence
look away

Green Boots n Lil Honeys

n i'm waitin for the light to turn green/
n i see these two fat kentucky fried oozie-lookin brothas/
peepin me like i'm the lil cutie/wantin to jump in
their long Sanford n Son lookin hooptie/
now i'm not one to judge or nothin/
but these two look like the kind who might/
give me a free flight into the wall/
jus cuz i'm not actin right/if you know what i mean
n they smilin at me/n i'm waitin for the light to turn green
n tryin to look like i'm real into the sidewalk/
cuz that's where it's at/n i can feel these brothas
jus waitin for me to hop into the back seat/
where the springs poppin out/all the time
i'm thinkin/why these folks lookin
like i want to get with them so bad

n all the time i'm thinkin of the videos
you know/where the brotha's in the beat up car/
drivin real slow/he got money/
but he don't put it into his car/
cuz Oakland Police stop him twice as many times a night
if he had somethin like a BMW/cuz they know
if he got a dope car he a dope dealer/
anyway/it's kinda makin sense now/
cuz it's kinda in style for lil honeys
to be all over somebody big who look like
somethin white people call the police on
cuz they jus look wrong/
n honeys be all over them in like twos n threes
sometimes/in the videos/i know you seen them/
so what i'm sayin is it's kinda in style to be kissin
n huggin n rubbin on somebody
who knock you out in a minute/

31

but still give you money to get ya nails done/
it's hip you know/in style n shit/
n i'm not one who don't like style
cuz i'm lookin kinda fly
in my knee green boots and black raiders jacket/
but you know style ain't what you see on tv

n all the time these brothas think imma get with them/
cuz they the B-boys/n they been gettin some play/
n they been thinkin they can get some more
from this here honey on the corner/well
i'm jus not that much in style

n the light turns green n they cruise by real slow/
makin sure i get a good look
at em/but you know the sidewalk is what's happenin/
i told you that already/
i pretend i don't see em but i shoulda screamed on em/
SEE YOU IN THE VIDEOS/that i turn on when i'm tired
of lookin at that damn news/you know/
where war is kinda in style/
green boots n gas masks/you know/
how in high school the recruiter rolls by/
talkin bout how you can earn money/
get a education/see the world/n people hop in cuz
these folks tryin to get where they goin/wherever that is/
n they seen on tv that it's kinda in style to hop on over
to somethin that will fuck you up in a minute/
n they didn't really know it would be like that/
tryin to find a way out from where they're at/
n somebody drive by offerin all this kinda shit/
n they think it's kinda cool cuz you know/
on tv it's kinda cool to be a soldier/kinda in style/
n the big dealers just sittin up there/
thinkin you be their lil honey
or somethin/n i wonder why
they think i be down for somethin like that/why
we be down for somethin like that/
n i think it's cuz it's in style or somethin

like biker shorts n gold teeth n Ray Bans
to cover a black eye/
everybody seem like they down for alla that
cuz nobody say nothin different/
n i don't neither/i jus keep on waitin on the green light

Backdraft

I had to stay up like the smoke above the sirens
you are the blood we need
I had to stay up with the pens crying
I don't know how to cry for you but you are hot on my skin

I don't know fires
just the ones in my head with no chorus
the flames crawl out of my television
the crosses burn good

n if Kingsford lights faster
Nike can make us do it
n Uh Huh is high vocabulary

I don't wonder that twelve people could think
what they seen is not what they seen
I don't wonder how bats turn to whiffles
n rollin on the ground is enough to scare all them men
n them bats is really blind doves
n a belly rollin on the ground is a powerful position

now you are my tv screen
how does it feel to have fire serenade you at night
I might call you Rosa but you did not mean to get your rib
    broke
on my account
I might call you right on time but you did not know the
    revolution
was waiting
windows burst for you n uncles die in your name

you brought fire from out of my closet n under my bed
you are large as my tv screen but you cannot fight
      my monsters crawling
in doves clothing they are bigger than my house
the cross burns my front yard n smoke over the roof chants
      your name
the sirens rise
cuz you are the blood we need

What Will It Take?

I spoke to Mother Earth this morning
I said
"Mamma
I'm afraid
I'm not gonna have no children
till there's
no more war."
She said to me
"Honey
I'm afraid
I'm not gonna have no more war
till there's
no more children."

Cesarean Section

In a chamber of razor black glass
Truth sings without mercy

You squeeze your calves
and rest your head upon your knees
your body a fetal rocking chair
wrapped in crimson silk
back and forth, forth and back
silence's lullaby sings without mercy

And those of vision
you hear their voices
call from just beyond the glass
to join them

Who pushed their souls
to finally cry out
each utterance a weapon
to avenge
to sing the songs of voices lost
to sting with songs
those who must be held accountable

And those of vision
you taste their world
clear fear
severe enough to burn your lungs
their silver knives scare you
the pain is ice and slices
you will suffocate
you cannot cry out it is not your time

And so rock back and forth, forth and back
to Truth's screeching lullaby
in a waiting chamber
where a congregation of watchguards
call from just beyond the glass
to join them

Are you not yet ready to be born into their army?

In a womb of razor black glass
O Truth sings without mercy without and within
you cannot resist any longer.

A Split Tree
Still Grows

Haiku I

Sometimes I wonder
why did I have to be Black
I get over it

Blues Poem I

but you need to tell me why you don want no paid holiday
said you need to tell me why you don want no paid holiday
a country starve for liberty done push the plate away

Martin's holiday so wrong you vote to work instead
Black man's holiday so wrong you vote to work instead
denyin one who fought for liberty cuz it waz Blackfolks
that he led

Labels for 99cent

Who passin them out
on the corner for dirt cheap
Labels for 99cent
Whitewash Militant Bitch Hoe Oreo
Nigga Gangsta Hoogie Bougie Ultra Black Ultra Wack
Labels for 99cent
Who passin them out
on the corner for dirt cheap
and
Who buyin them up so quick
Who puttin them on they T-shirts
and slappin them on they brotha's back
like these labels was made to order
buyin them up so quick
Like 99cent a straight up bargain.

In a Darkroom

Blackisblackisblackisblack.
Pitch black.

You wind the undeveloped film of future around a steel reel
a prophet purpose at the age of 21.
Your voice to keep me company
shakes the solution while explaining the process.

Jah
my sister
love all but the white man
who destroy the balance of the earth.
Will exterminate his devil ass off this planet
like Lucifer from the city of angels.
And we will aid him
in his glorious mission.

Know
this science this knowledge this truth.

And I stand next to your discipline.
My mind like the film wraps around
I cannot understand I cannot understand I cannot
understand.

I pull your wisdom from the solution. My brother
it too clearly reproduces race history in the negative.
I cannot dig your knowledge
but I dig your sincerity in your quest for peace.

Jah guidance.
Peace my sister.
You will soon see the truth.

My larynx swings open.

The balance of this earth
is not dependent upon the absence of devils
it is dependent upon the presence of angels and
spirit, not color, determines.

Blind, you mutter to yourself
as you prepare Kodak paper.

Yes.
My eyes cannot find the truth to which you bear witness.

But accompany me to the door with respect for
my brother is always my brother.
The door swings shut on a whispered duet
Jah guidance.

I Want to Hear Your Genius

for Joshua

We are in a pulling
I wait for your words while
your eyes blink too fast for normal
your lips work too hard for your voice to catch up

We are in a room growing hot
I don't hear them laughing

I pray for your genius
in a pulling of words
already defeated

I Will Speak Genius to Myself

So tired of trying to prove myself
analyticalphilosophicalintellectually
know what I mean?
Those epistemologicaterminal terms dammit
clutter my mind. Styrofoam words.

What happened to
using your own words
as long as you made yourself understood?
Now
I must recite flawlessly
another's vocabulary
before I can make sense in my own.
When I was a child
people understood me by watching my bright eyes
and butterfly hands.
In the academy I suppose
some white man taught everyone
to go blind—
to memorize terminology
to clap for words
seen as academic
to refuse one whose words are not.

And they learned their lesson well
for the audition is over
and there remains a brown girl
in the middle of a polished wooden floor.

And so here I am
lighting a disappointed cigarette
in the middle of the stage
the wooden stage

polishedreallyshiny
really fucking shiny
with absolutely no scratches on it.

I can see my brown face in the reflection
but no one else is here so no one else can see it
Doesn't matter anyway
I'm sure someone would say
that it is not an authentic face
because it's defined in a brown polished floor context
which is of course
outside of a grey rough concrete context
which is of course
really the only context for a face like mine.

But I know that my face is authentic
my mind is authentic
my words are authentic
so I will speak genius to myself.

Satisfied I snub my cigarette in the waxy finish
and stroll off the empty stage
to my concrete context

It's too bad that no one will ever know
what was in the brown image; after I'm gone
all they will see
is that old cigarette burn in the middle of their
very very shiny wood floor.

Stoplight Politics

check out
sista
on de corner
bar-b-q Fritos Fanta soda
dookie braids
knee-high boots
Raiders jacket
gold tooth
talkin shit

she embarrass you huh

go head sista
roll on by
you
rollin somewhere
you
gon conquer the nation
worl in yo hand
wich yo education

you
better den sista
on de corner
thank god
you never did hang wit de brothas
goin nowhere
talkin shit
waitin for de light to turn green

go head
turn yo head

look straight ahead
n roll that Lexus home
to yo fifty g man hundred g crib

pray for de light ta turn green
befo you look back ova
one more time
n realize
you both de same thang
hopin on de same thang

you jus got a car

Revolution Song
from a Future Cockroach

for Pya

We sit
five in a small room
green rug
we study
a sistas n brothas
everyday America

n i just wanna share somethin wit you

some young people comin up soon
n i advise you be ready

cuz
we sit
five in a small room
discussin multi-million dollar
corporations
n Tamara say:

i step on any white man
in my path
to gain power for my people
n not only step on him
but stomp him so deep in the ground
that the next person
walk smooth over his back
to join me

i will step on so many folks
to sly get us to the top
that when i die
God will reincarnate me

as a cockroach
to get me back

but i bet in the world i create
i be a cockroach
on a
white person
wall

n we five
in a small room
green rug
believe her
cuz we all know
we
hate the smell of Raid

Haiku II

Memories come down
and me once again
caught without an umbrella.

Souls

To my seven years she thundered
"Don't you go into that grove at night
there's spirits up in them trees you know."
I shivered in the sheets for seven more.

At winking eyes in fluttering leaves and
faces on my bedroom door
souls

in trees.

My scarred up black living room chair
I crawled into it sometimes
curled sideways like upon Daddy's lap
taken by the singing

My cheek against it's cool back
rockers creaking me the history
of trees.

I found the soul within Ebony
wise.
And rocking
surrounded by souls
like the one holding me.
Look. The door's watching.
Listen. The desk's humming.

Grove

I bring you trees

Mahogany
laquered blood drying

Pecan
sweet cream melting

Oak
incensed musk burning

Ebony
silence.

Surrounded by trees
We stand among a chained nation
changed from trunks to lumber to objects
souls live
alive

Behold your living room

Mahogany
laquered blood drying

Pecan
sweet cream melting

Oak
incensed musk burning

Ebony
black silence.

The Call

Tossing in a white linen ocean
Mistress is drowning in dread again.
Come out of the quarters this evening Tobiah
My sheets grow cold without you.

Tossing in a white linen ocean
Mistress is fighting the fear again
Don't leave my love tonight Tobiah
My heart grows cold without you.

Mistress is calling on God again
Mistress is fading from faith.

Tossing in a white linen ocean
Mistress is gasping for pride again
Falling from grace from race Tobiah
Her heart grows cold.

Mistress

Why you shining so bright in my living room?
Bitch
you know I'll slap that glow right off your face.

Miss Pecan cream your neck so high and back so straight
You think you're a model
as you model
my dress, my shoes, my stockings.

I'd break both your legs but bring me the milk
I'd chop off your arms but
go shell the peas
I'd twist off your breasts but
go nurse my baby
I'd burn off your ears
are you listening to me?

Well, all I can do is dull you with spit
and make you shine brighter in heaven.

A Split Tree Still Grows

Look at me
I am old
I am the beginning
I survive the seasons

spring
found me alive with wealth of earth
strangers wanted my branches
cut chained and transported over oceans
cargo in airless chamber
grafted in new soil

but my roots, my roots
held tight to my soul
nothing could shake them

summer
lightning lashed and cracked
split my chapped bark
licked through flesh
sap oozed down

but my roots, my roots
held tight to my soul
nothing could shake them

fall
forced my branches to bear fruit
bruised and beaten and mangled
they dangled for days upon my limbs
until the rotting rope gave in

but my roots, my roots
held tight to my soul
nothing could shake them

winter
rain poured down
from thunder's hooves in white sheets
hurricanes blew me
from the south to the north, east to the west
but I did not break
I bent and bowed to weather the storm

and my roots, my roots
held tight to my soul
nothing could shake them

Look at me
I am chained whipped lynched and split
still I grow

still I rise and multiply
stretch and spread my arms wide
across the oceans
I am so large that
anthropologists and sociologists
study my arms over tea
they conclude my limbs alone are trees
their foolish science
eclipses me
one tree

my spirit passes on
through young tender branches
as they create new life on foreign soil
leaves with red yellow purple undertones
sing the sun drink the rain sway the wind pray the sky
for justice

until they
dry and withered
retire to the earth

but you see
their devotion determination
blood and prayers
they are nutrition
that seeps deep down into the ground
and the roots reach
into the soil
I say my roots, my roots
grab down to the soul
and nothing can shake them
because
with each struggle
I grow stronger

Look at me
I am we
we are old
we are the beginning of life
we survive the seasons
we are the new buds upon the highest branches
we reach outward to new places and
reach upward to new goals
and nothing can shake us
because our souls, I say our souls
grab down to the roots
as we reach upward to the sky.

We Are the
Young Magicians

At Least Once a Week

dedicated to Smell This

sisters
light one stick of jasmine incense
and seven mulberry candles
in the bathroom
with the lights out

sing
magenta to yourself
as you step into the bathtub
create new verses
to scrub the pain out of your hair

soak in your letters
just ten more minutes
til your exhausted fingers
wrinkle

then
completely cleansed
step out
dry yourself off
to withstand the cold air

don't
wash the tub
let the magic linger
into a ring
of unified voices

blow out the candles
the incense glows
and smell
in the darkness
our power

In the Mirror Too Long

Mamma
ever since i was small
you say

"don let me catch you
in the mirror too long
you know God don like vain"

but Mamma
um 22 now n
still nobody say
pretty look like
me

n Mamma
if i don
look in the mirror
once in a while
n tell me
um beautiful

i waste
ma whole life
searchin the city over
for somebody
who will

You So Woman

for Anya

lady
when ya purple heels hit concrete
afros swing
cool jazz hot baby
strollin by cry amen

so holy
preachas stutta
thighs so righteous
pews jump up n catch the spirit n
hymns speak in tongues

so sweet
bees leave the daffodils behind
for honey you make table sugar taste sour n
Mrs. Butterworth sho can't find a damn thing to say
when you aroun

lookin so good
cockroaches ask you to step on em
sos they can see heaven
befo
and after they die n

you love ya people so much
if you was on pilgrimage
the Sahara Desert would run to the Atlantic
jus to make sure you don't get thirsty n
camels would kiss you for choosin they back

but Africa don't got you
we do n glad too

so girl
you jus keep on
makin the sunset procrastinate n
givin the rainbows a complex
you a silk earthquake
you a velvet hurricane
n girl you so woman
i be damn
if you don't put a full moon to shame.

El Ser Mujer

To be a woman
is to lose all your children but one
and still be able to stand in the shower

to chop onions and let yourself cry full
to remember your babies' favorite recipes
and cook them

to be a woman is to forgive yourself
the wrong steps
create new ones
as you learn to love heavy brows

to be a woman is to look in the mirror
to make your single bed day after day
and iron your pants perfect white crease perfect

to let the tides come when they are ready
let God hold you when your head is almost below water
to sing
to sing in the shower childless but one
and standing

Blues Poem II

o chile what imma leave you when i
o chile what mamma leave you when she gone
n how's my sweet brown sugar gonna get along

o baby mamma give to you her
here baby mamma give to you her song
God inside ma heart will keep me strong

Momma

You taste like thick cream and almonds in your prayers
for God to watch over your children
I think of you every time I drink coffee
angels sashaying in the steam
bring memories full as the moon and slow grace
I send my love spinning
into your palms together
the palace of angels and where I find shelter.

Rescue from the Dance of
One Hundred Mermaids

Still water I'm seeing
from the granite beside the sea
calm blue at first glance
but somewhere within
I sense red

Still eyes I'm seeing
from the granite beside the sea
"The soul it flows in peace" I say
but somewhere within
I sense turbulence

I want to wade in
but perhaps
coral sharpened
by years of storm
will slice my steps
if I don't place my sole correctly
on the sea floor

I want to swim
but perhaps
undercurrents
will overcome my stroke if I don't
parallel tide rhythms
quick enough

I will not wade in
I will not wade in

I remain among the granite
peering into placid blue

I will not be drowned by
self-centered undertides

I will not wade in

But the sea
makes me want to kiss the periwinkle pulse
and despite all caution
I let loose my shadow
to slowly descend the rocks
to glide upon the surface
to dance on blue

Sweet cool smooth my shadow moves
the dance of one hundred mermaids
and just as I am about to enter
my shadow cries out

The water suddenly
surging my emissary into hostage
crimson tide pools swirling
my shadow into unrecognizable shapes
breakers erupting blood red whispers
"I will tear you apart!"

Dancing the ego dance to show
a shadow of myself
how powerful is the sea
working to drown me
in order to impress me

Spitting magnificent sprays of salt upon the rocks
which leave a bitter taste in my mouth
for I realize
I came to bathe
in the power of a sea
that refuses to know the beauty of my dance

My shadow cries out
Tides try to choke and stifle it
to create a like image of other torn mermaids
but I will not let my shadow be destroyed

I rise from the granite
and call upon
my grace my youth my wisdom my strength
to employ every part
of that which I am endowed

Mind calculates
brow smoothes
eyes clear
muscles tighten
toes pointed
I fly

A crystal clear arrow
rescuing my shadow upon the waves at 45 degrees
without even a ripple
slicing through blue through red
                        red through blue
I glide
arm over then under, over then under

I dive and stroke
with determination to be whole
and with each stroke
I leave behind
a rippling current
of purple.

Haiku III

It only takes a phone call
to trip up my groove

just when i thought i could dance

Today You Dial Me

my "hello" roll heavy when i answer the phone
cuz back in the day
Daddy don't want
a high girl voice
Daddy want
a low make sense kinda voice
a storm roll heavy
get Daddy attention
n back in the day
princes from the projects
greet my downtown behind
with how
you doin
a reply roll heavy
keep
the princes at the projects
from steppin to my side
n yesterday
i challenge a professor
that expect less from a black girl
my tone roll heavy
command respect
n yesterday
my brothers
discuss revolution
my opinion roll heavy
make them listen
my octave
roll away
feeble woman
my octave
make way

for my words my colors my numbers
my sisters

and brother
today you dial me
my "hello" roll heavy when i answer
and brother
you say
girl, you sound sooo sexy
and brother
yeah brother
yeah brother

    my octave moan for you
punk

A Woman's Scent

is more like roses
drying on the wall of a kitchen
tokens of the ones who left

is more like kale and cardamom
wild mint weathered gloves cinnamon
and thyme

if you listen you can catch it in the eyes
waiting for the right one
to take it away
the roses the garlic and onion peeling

a hand to open the windows she pretends
never existed
all that simmers outside her kitchen
and a promise of locks to where she's been.

Marriage and
the 18-Hour Bra

I hear
men prefer
heavy chested women
well that's just fine
cuz I got
such a load on my chest
I feel more mule than woman
and I wouldn't mind one lil bit
in fact
I'd be much obliged
if some man asked me
if he could
take it all off

Blues Poem III

las nite you said you'd bring me the moon
o las nite you said you'd bring me the moon
but tomorrow imma get me the sun
if you don't fetch it soon

cuz all you bring today is bruises and scars
yeah all you give today is bruises and scars
and ma cryin eyes too swoll
to wish on stars

I Hold a Cave
in the Palm of My Hand

My hand you once call delicate
hold a cave
that will be a fist tomorrow

today
you and the smell of new women
may crawl in to leave my afternoon forever

today
you may throw in your fist and angry tongue
and 40 ounce

today
you may throw in your steel toe boots and shatter glass
and teeth and plates broke and heat and glass pipe
and back door banging

today
you may crawl in this cave
if you can
and come out naked as yesterday
when your eyes were real
and love was a safe place
if you want a safe place
cuz I need a safe place

I hold a cave in the palm of my hand
growing smaller.

A Chorus of Needles
Singing away the Thirst

if anything it is ice in my veins rushing for the door
and knives holding my head
my feet won't move
my eyes don't see nothing
not black not red
if anything the devil is behind me and coming
I could heave myself into the morning
but there is no time
my voice rolls from my stomach like lava
but falls in ashes from my lips
there is no one to catch me but God in his grace
and a strong flush of angels

Up Sister

Jus get your beautiful black behind up
off that cold Armstrong tile

Don't you give up
jus cuz you don't see nowhere to go
We have faith in you

You are brilliant and bold
like nobody I have ever seen before
How the hell you think you got this far anyway?

Can't do it no more huh
too tired . . . too achin
to arch to the ceilin one more time
Jus to find you back on the floor tomorrow

Girl don't you know that floor got
the change that fell out my pocket
when I was huggin my knees by the corner last night?
And Bessie's birth control
and Billie's Marlboros
and mascara and matches and mace
and everything else you could find
in a woman's pockets that fall out
when she collapses with a hundred-pound sigh

But you know how we leave that floor?
Some hand reaches in that darkness
and pulls you up by the waist
even when you don't want to go
cuz it has faith in you

See you got to get up cuz you're Us
and when you fall We get bruised

Sometimes you can't do it by yourself
but you got a hand reachin out right now
Don't you know
you got a hundred hands
from every single Black woman who claims that floor

Yes you'll find yourself here again
But for now
jus worry bout gettin your beautiful black bchind up
off that cold Armstrong tile
And don't worry bout that lipstick sittin by your corner
I'll get it next time I'm here.

9am for Shange

a black woman love bite
i feel scare n try to hide it/but it won go
so i get mad at u/this mornin
cuz u givin me a gif/that refuse to be refuse
u show me/don be silent
u show everybody my bizness/it hurt me
the moan rise/the blood rush to my neck
a black woman love bite/it hurt me/i slam the door

cuz um not really wantin nobody to see my bizness
i be scare/somebody see my stuff/n run off wit it/
like they always do
cuz they know it in a black woman
i be hidin my pain/in my ulcer/n i dance
22 years/n folk still tryin to run off wit alla my stuff
u love so much/u bite
my neck/bend 45 degree lookin at the groun
cuz not much to look at above the sidewalk most days
i walk/to the corner store/9am/to get the anger out
i count the cracks/see a penny on the groun/dark n ol
n ugly
how it get like that/cuz no other money turn like that
n i member what a penny look like new/glow
like sunset color
how it get like that/how it get like that . . .

panties torn bloody slimy jheri curl juice in my ear . . .
mr. w. four fat finger han tryin to grab my lef tittie
n the other han on the steerin wheel
gettin me to school on time . . . baby
i really wanna go wit you to the clinic but u know
i be real busy u be alright call me . . .

he in a meeting miss please call again
tomorrow call again tomorrow call again tomorrow. . . .

9am/this mornin/i get mad at you
for givin me a gif/that refuse to be refuse
n now i cant hold no more/the ulcer wit a smile
my bizness glow on my neck/sunset color like

copper/use to be precious maybe/someplace
everybody love it treasure it/n everybody know
it worth somethin
but copper not worth nothin/not on my block
cuz there a lotta pennies jus chillin on the groun
lookin beat up n mean
muss be cuz a penny only got one cent
my frien tell me rub some acid on it and it burn
the glow back out sunset color
how it spose to be/use to be/so beautiful

um sorry i get mad at u this mornin
cuz u too busy las nite/speakin yo love/to realize
you givin me a gif/that scare me to acknowledge/
it don go away
n so i have to see it love it
cuz it become a part of me from /n well/i am
n u beautiful/therefore
it be beautiful/what i see
u show me/sing myself n love her fiercely/it burn
like acid
but i see me glow in the mirror/sunset color/
i refuse to be refuse
i love it/part of me from u/me from u/me n u
therefore it
beautiful

We Are the Young Magicians

Go sit yo ass down
we don't need no volunteers
to disappear
from a box trap door
a hole in the floor
we reappear
folks you never seen before
reach deep
behind black velvet curtains

we don't need no trick cane
to amaze
with a mere wave of the pen
we transform grey concrete
to yellow brick roads

we don't pull no rabbits
from a hat
we pull rainbows
from a trash can
we pull hope
from the dictionary
n teach it how to ride the subway

we don't guess the card in yo hand
we know it
aim to change it
yeah
we know magic
and don't be so sure that card in yo hand
is the Ace